Craft Co

Become a Master Bartender with 54 Quick, Easy and Affordable Recipes for Your Best Parties

Copyright Notice

Table of Contents

Foreword 10

Chapter One: Tools, Ingredients, and Techniques for Making Great
Cocktails 15

Chapter Two: 18 Modern and Affordable Alcoholic Cocktails 20

Creamsicle Martini...22

White Russian with Pumpkin Spice 24

Christmas Eggnog Martini...26

Cookie Dough Martini...28

Grape Cosmopolitan 30

The Grown-Up Cherry Coke 32

Whiskey Ginger 34

Sweet Pumpkin Spice Rum 36

Sour Apple Daiquiri 38

Black Cherry Snow Cone...40

Coconut Mango Tango 42

Strawberry Ginger Ale...44

Gin Fizz with Sloe Gin...46

Halloween Candy Corn Margarita...48

Spicy Jalapeno Margarita 50

Amaretto Bourbon..52

Honey Cake Cocktail 53

Bourbon and Ginger...55

Candy Cane Hot Cocoa..59

Whipped Cream Hot Chocolate..61

Aged Hot Toddy 63

Coffee with a Kick..65

Buttered Hot Coffee 67

Cocoa with a Kick...69

Atomic Cider 71

Bourbon Brandy Yuzu 73

Cinnamon Coffee Cocktail...75

Minted Cocoa...77

Spiced Buttered Rum 79

Dark Cinnamon Rum Hot Cocoa 81

Almond Hot Coffee 83

Spiced Bourbon Cider 85

Jim's Hot Cocoa 87

Buttered Clove Rum...89

Cloved Whiskey 91

Cinnamon Cocoa Cocktail...93

Chapter Four: 18 Tasty Non-Alcoholic Cocktails 95

Cranberry Cooler...97

Fruit Cream Soda 99

Virgin Strawberry Mojito...101

Coke and Grenadine 103

Raspberry Fizz Bomb 105

Cranberry Sparkle..107

Virgin Mint Colada 109

Lime and Coconut Virgin Martini 111

Virgin Champagne Cocktail 113

Sherbert Mojitos 115

Ginger Cherry Virgin Cocktail 117

Apple Citrus Cocktail 119

Cucumber Grape Refresher 121

Honey Watermelon Slushie 123

Citrus Berry Cocktail 125

Cranberry Apple Fizz 127

Mango Refresher 129

Sweet Grenadine 131

Best Practices & Common Mistakes 133

Conclusion 136

Foreword

"If you were to ask me if I'd ever had the bad luck to miss my daily cocktail, I'd have to say that I doubt it; where certain things are concerned, I plan ahead."
– Luis Bunuel

I enjoy a good cocktail and I make no secret of it. There is something deliciously self-indulgent about coming home from a hard day at work, mixing a cocktail, and taking the time to unwind.

Over the years, however, I have become somewhat dissatisfied with the usual cocktail choices. I mastered the martini and subjugated the sours, but the same old flavor profiles became mundane. I found myself bored with the one timeslot I set aside for myself on a daily basis.

In an effort to put a little spark back into my "me time", I decided to venture into unknown territory. I started to mix my own craft cocktails.

When I first began coming up with craft cocktail concepts I felt like something of a mad scientist. I'd throw together ingredients, taste the outcome, add a little more of this and a splash of that...until eventually, I mastered a taste profile that had a little something special. I repeated this process more times than I care to remember until I came up with a series of pretty damn good cocktail recipes.

In the chapters that follow, you will find some of those recipes. I hope that you enjoy drinking them as much as I do.

Bonus: Your FREE Gift

As a token of our appreciation, please take advantage of the **FREE Gift** - a lifetime **VIP Membership** at our book club.

Follow the link below to download your FREE books:

http://bit.ly/vipbookclub

As a VIP member, you will get an instant **FREE** access to exclusive new releases and bestselling books.

Chapter One: Tools, Ingredients, and Techniques for Making Great Cocktails

"A penny saved is a cocktail earned!"
– Anon

The Tools You Need to Make a Great Cocktail

When it comes to making a really great cocktail, there are a few tools that every home bartender must keep on hand. These tools are for more than appearances, they help to ensure a tasty and well-mixed drink every time you mix!

- A jigger – a jigger helps to measure accurate quantities of liquid to make sure a cocktail is made using the right ratios of ingredients.

- A muddler – used to muddle together ingredients for a cocktail.

- A shaker – necessary to combine and thoroughly mix together liquid ingredients of a cocktail that needs to be shaken.

- A strainer – used with a shaker to strain a drink into a glass. The strainer is also useful for cocktails that use solid ingredients for flavoring.

- A spoon – not just a spoon, but a cocktail spoon. This long handled spoon enables stirring cocktails in even the most peculiar-shaped glass.

The Ingredients You Need to Make Great Cocktails

With the right tools on hand to make a cocktail, the next thing to stock up on is ingredients! Not every cocktail is going to use the same ingredients, but there are some core ingredients that you will use on a regular basis so it's best to stock up.

- Your basic liquors - these will vary depending on what YOU like to drink most. There's no point stocking what you won't drink. Think of the staples like gin, vodka, scotch, whiskey, and rum. Just don't overstock or your money will go to waste!

- Mixers – club soda, tonic water, soda, and fruit juice. Again, these will be to YOUR taste or to accommodate your guests in moderation.

- Garnishes – cherries, lemons, limes, olives. Some of these are going to be perishable so you can only stock up so far ahead of time. Other garnishes, like olives, for example, will store for a long time and are always good to keep behind the bar.

- Bitters – bitters are used to flavor drinks. Pick your bitters based on the drinks you make most often. While bitters will last a long time in storage, there is no point throwing money away!

- Ice – if you don't have an ice maker, make sure that you store plenty of ice ahead of time because it is most definitely a necessity!

- Glassware – if you want to get fancy, invest in a set of each variety of drinking glasses (highball glasses, rocks glasses, martini glasses, etc.) but keep in mind that unless you're having cocktail parties every weekend, you can make do with a couple of each glass variety.

Techniques for Making Great Cocktails

With your bar stocked up for a moderate get together, you need to know a little something about making a good cocktail. There are a million and one tips I could give you when it comes to good cocktail mixing, but let's stick with the basics to get you started.

- Add your mixers FIRST and your alcohol LAST. This makes screwing up a drink much less expensive!

- Follow the recipe! Don't improvise, cocktail recipes are delicately balanced to bring out the best in all of the ingredients!

- MIX YOUR DRINKS! If you don't stir or shake your cocktails your final sip is going to be one incredible surprise! Mix your drinks well to get a good and uninformed flavor.

- More liquor does NOT make a better drink. Overdoing the liquor offsets the balance I mentioned before and results in a poorly mixed and badly tasting drink.

- Avoid overshaking a cocktail by looking at the edges of the ice. When the edges of your ice cubes begin to smooth, your cocktail is mixed.

- Always strain drinks that have seeded ingredients like berries.

- Don't use your best liquor for mixing cocktails. The good stuff should be savored for taste alone, don't take away from that flavor by mixing. On that note, don't use the cheapest liquor for mixing either, it'll leave your cocktails tasting like paint remover.

- Shake your citrus and stir your booze. This is the general rule of thumb when it comes to shaking or stirring cocktails. Yes, it does make a difference!

- Make sure your ice is pure and filtered. There is nothing worse than a good cocktail with badly flavored ice!

Chapter Two: 18 Modern and Affordable Alcoholic Cocktails

"A cocktail done right can really show your guests that you care."
– Danny Meyer

In this chapter, you will learn how to make the following modern and affordable alcoholic cocktails:

- Creamsicle Martini

- White Russian with Pumpkin Spice

- Christmas Eggnog Martini

- Cookie Dough Martini

- Grape Cosmopolitan

- The Grown-Up Cherry Coke

- Whiskey Ginger

- Sweet Pumpkin Pie Rum

- Sour Apple Daiquiri

- Black Cherry Snow Cone

- Coconut Mango Tango

- Strawberry Ginger Ale

- Gin Fizz with Sloe Gin

- Halloween Candy Corn Margarita

- Spicy Jalapeno Margarita

- Amaretto Bourbon

- Honey Cake Cocktail

- Bourbon and Ginger

Creamsicle Martini

Staple Liquor	Vodka
Flavor	Fruity, Sweet

Ingredients

- 1 part crème de cocoa white liqueur

- 2 parts orange whipped vodka

- 2 parts orange juice

- Orange wedges for garnish

- Ice

- Chilled martini glass

Let's Mix:

1. Add your ice to a shaker and pour your orange juice, crème de cocoa white liqueur, and vodka over the ice in that order.

2. Put the lid on your shaker and shake until you open the shaker and see that the edges of your ice have smoothed.

3. Strain your cocktail into a chilled martini glass and add a wedge of orange to the side of the glass!

Extra Tip:

Orange whipped vodka can be difficult to find, try looking for the brand name Pinnacle and you should find it without any trouble.

White Russian with Pumpkin Spice

Staple Liquor	Vodka
Flavor	Sweet

Ingredients

- 3 parts whipped vodka

- 1 part coffee liqueur

- ¼ part pumpkin puree

- 2 parts milk

- 1 part pumpkin spice liquid coffee creamer

- Dash pumpkin spice

- Ice

- Tall glass

Let's Mix:

1. In a tall glass, add your creamer, puree, liqueur, and vodka. Stir with a tall spoon until your ingredients are well mixed.

2. Carefully add ice to your glass.

3. Pour your milk on top of your cocktail.

4. Garnish with a sprinkle of the pumpkin pie spice and serve.

Extra Tip:

This is a very sweet cocktail and best served as an after dinner drink or as a "before bed" drink.

Christmas Eggnog Martini

Staple Liquor	Vodka
Flavor	Sweet

Ingredients

- 1 part vodka

- 1 part amaretto liqueur

- 2 parts eggnog

- Nutmeg

- Ice

- Chilled martini glass

Let's Mix:

1. Add your ice to a shaker and pour your eggnog, amaretto, and vodka over it in that order.

2. Shake your ingredients in your shaker and strain into your chilled martini glass.

3. Sprinkle your nutmeg on top and serve!

Extra Tip:

Be careful not to overdo the nutmeg or you will throw off the whole flavor profile of this cocktail. Just use a sprinkling – enough to flavor, but not so much that the top of your cocktail is covered.

Cookie Dough Martini

Staple Liquor	Vodka
Flavor	Sweet

Ingredients

- 1 part cookie dough flavored vodka

- 1 part half and half

- Cookie sprinkles

- Vanilla icing

- 1 maraschino cherry

- Ice

- Chilled martini glass

Let's Mix:

1. Lightly rim your chilled martini glass with the vanilla icing and then dip in the sprinkles to rim the glass with them.

2. Put your ice in a shaker and then pour your half and half over the ice. Add your vodka. Shake until your ice edges smooth.

3. Strain your cocktail over the ice and add a cherry to your glass to garnish before serving.

Extra Tip:

Cookie dough vodka is another one made by Pinnacle. I haven't found another brand that offers it as of yet.

Grape Cosmopolitan

Staple Liquor	Vodka
Flavor	Fruity

Ingredients

- 1 part triple sec liqueur

- ½ part raspberry schnapps liqueur

- 2 parts grape vodka

- Orange slices

- Ice

- Chilled martini glass

Let's Mix:

1. Add your ice to a shaker and pour your raspberry schnapps, triple sec, and vodka over it. Shake until your ice edges smooth.

2. Strain your martini into your chilled martini glass and garnish the edge of the glass with a slice of orange.

Extra Tip:

A delicious berry rich cocktail, this is the perfect drink for a cocktail party at any time of the year. Add a twist to this one by replacing the raspberry schnapps with a mixed berry schnapps instead.

The Grown-Up Cherry Coke

Staple Liquor	Vodka
Flavor	Sweet

Ingredients

- 2 parts cherry vodka

- 2 parts Coke

- 1 maraschino cherry

- Ice

- Rocks glass

Let's Mix:

1. Add your ice to the rocks glass and pour your Coke over it.

2. Add your cherry vodka to the coke and stir gently.

3. Garnish your glass with a cherry and serve!

Extra Tip:

Add a dash of vanilla syrup to this cocktail to
make a grown-up vanilla cherry coke!

Whiskey Ginger

Staple Liquor	Irish Whiskey
Flavor	Sweet

Ingredients

- 1 part ginger whiskey

- 2 parts ginger ale

- Lime wedges

- Lemon wedges

- Ice

- Collins glass

Let's Mix:

1. Add your ice to the Collins glass and pour your Irish whiskey over it.

2. Fill the rest of your glass with ginger ale.

3. Garnish your glass with lemon and lime and serve!

Extra Tip:

Skip the lemon and lime wedges and garnish this one with candied ginger instead!

Sweet Pumpkin Spice Rum

Staple Liquor	Rum, Vodka
Flavor	Sweet

Ingredients

- 1 part Cruzan Velvet Cinn Rum

- 1 part pumpkin pie vodka

- Cinnamon sugar

- Ice

- Shot glass

Let's Mix:

1. Carefully wet the rim of a shot glass and dip it in your cinnamon sugar.

2. Add your ice to a shaker and pour your rum and vodka over it. Shake to combine.

3. Strain your cocktail into your shot glass and serve.

Extra Tip:

If you like things extra sweet, top your shot glass with whipped cream.

Sour Apple Daiquiri

Staple Liquor	Rum
Flavor	Sour

Ingredients

- 1 part aged dark rum

- ½ part sour apple schnapps

- 1 part apple juice

- 1 part sour mix

- 1 scoop vanilla ice cream

- 1 pineapple wedge

- Daquiri glass

Let's Mix:

1. Add your ice cream to your blender and pour your apple juice, sour mix, schnapps, and rum over it.

2. Blend until completely smooth and pour into your daiquiri glass.

3. Garnish the edge of your glass with a piece of pineapple before serving.

Extra Tip:

Don't over blend this cocktail, you want to keep the thickness of the ice cream in the final drink.

Black Cherry Snow Cone

Staple Liquor	Rum
Flavor	Sweet

Ingredients

- 1 part black cherry rum

- 1 part cherry schnapps liqueur

- Lime wedges

- 1 mint sprig

- Crushed ice

- Rocks glass

Let's Mix:

1. Fill a rocks glass with crushed ice.

2. Pour your liqueur and rum over your crushed ice.

3. Add a squeeze of lime juice over your drink and garnish with your sprig of mint before serving.

Extra Tip:

Don't have mint on hand? You can garnish this one with a black cherry instead.

Coconut Mango Tango

Staple Liquor	Rum
Flavor	Fruity

Ingredients

- 1 part coconut rum

- 1 part mango rum

- 4 parts pineapple juice

- Ice

- Daiquiri glass

Let's Mix:

1. Add your ice to the daiquiri glass and pour in your pineapple juice.

2. Add your mango and coconut rums and stir gently.

3. Garnish the edge of your glass with a slice of pineapple and serve.

Extra Tip:

Freeze some mango cubes and add them to your glass along with your ice cubes for added flavor.

Strawberry Ginger Ale

Staple Liquor	Rum
Flavor	Sweet

Ingredients

- 12 parts strawberry rum

- 24 parts ginger ale

- 6 parts fresh lime juice

- 6 sprigs of rosemary

- Ice

- Punchbowl

- Rocks glass

Let's Mix:

1. Add your rum to the punch bowl and throw in your rosemary. Stir this mixture and let it stand.

2. After letting this mixture stand for a while to infuse the rum with your rosemary flavor, add in your lime juice. Put this bowl in the refrigerator to chill.

3. Once your ingredients are chilled, add ice to the punch bowl and pour in your ginger ale. Mix and then serve!

Extra Tip:

If desired, you can garnish this cocktail with a small sprig of rosemary. Just keep in mind that rosemary can be overpowering so don't go overboard!

Gin Fizz with Sloe Gin

Staple Liquor	Gin
Flavor	Sweet

Ingredients

- 1 ½ parts gin

- 1 ½ parts sloe gin

- 3 parts soda water

- 1 part lemon juice

- Lemon Slices

- Ice

- Tall glass

Let's Mix:

1. Add your ice to your tall glass.

2. Pour in your soda water and lemon juice. Next, add in your gin.

3. Stir gently to mix.

4. Garnish your glass with a slice of lemon and serve.

Extra Tip:

Make sure to use freshly squeezed lemon juice when making this cocktail. Artificial or bottled lemon juice will give this drink a very unpleasant taste.

Halloween Candy Corn Margarita

Staple Liquor	Tequila
Flavor	Sweet

Ingredients

- 8 parts light beer

- 6 parts agave tequila

- 3 parts triple sec

- 1 can frozen limeade

- 8 parts orange soda

- Orange sugar

- Pitcher

- Margarita glass

Let's Mix:

1. Add your limeade and orange soda to your pitcher and stir.

2. Add in your triple sec, tequila, and beer, and stir again.

3. Refrigerate your pitcher to chill.

4. Once your pitcher has chilled, take your margarita glass and wet the rim. Dip the wet rip in your orange sugar.

5. Pour your margarita and serve!

Extra Tip:

Orange sugar can be found at most craft stores that carry baking supplies. You can also find it more widely around Halloween.

Spicy Jalapeno Margarita

Staple Liquor	Tequila
Flavor	Fruity, Spicy

Ingredients

- 1 ½ parts agave tequila

- 1 ½ parts triple sec

- ½ part lime juice

- 2 sprigs cilantro

- 1 sliced jalapeno pepper

- Ice

- Tall glass

Let's Mix:

1. Add your lime juice, triple sec, and tequila to an ice filled shaker in that order. Throw in a single slice of jalapeno.

2. Shake until your ice edges smooth and then strain into an ice-filled tall glass.

3. Garnish your glass with the cilantro sprigs and serve.

Extra Tip:

Add extra garnish to this drink with an extra slice of jalapeno or lime.

Amaretto Bourbon

Staple Liquor	Bourbon
Flavor	Sweet

Ingredients

- ¾ part Bourbon

- ¾ part amaretto liqueur

- Shot glass

Let's Mix:

1. Pour your amaretto and bourbon into a shot glass and drink!

Extra Tip:

There is plenty to play with in this cocktail! Try alternating bourbon varieties to change your flavor profiles.

Honey Cake Cocktail

Staple Liquor	Vodka, Bourbon
Flavor	Sweet

Ingredients

- 1 part Jim Beam Honey

- 1 part King Cake vodka

- Sugar

- 2 parts lemon sour

- Lemon peel

- Chilled martini glass

Let's Mix:

1. In an ice-filled shaker, combine your ingredients and shake until the edges of the ice are smooth.

2. Dip the rim of your glass into water and rim it with sugar.

3. Strain the cocktail into the chilled martini glass.

4. Garnish with lemon peel before serving.

Extra Tip:

This is a delicious cocktail, but the liquors used are very particular so I don't recommend mixing this cocktail unless you are holding an event where you will use more than a drinks worth of ingredients.

Bourbon and Ginger

Staple Liquor	Bourbon
Flavor	Sweet

Ingredients

- 2 parts bourbon

- ½ part lime juice

- 2 ½ parts mango nectar

- 1 dash bitters

- ½ part ginger beer

- Mango cubes

- Cocktail glass

Let's Mix:

1. In a cocktail shaker with ice, combine your nectar, bourbon, ginger beer, lime, and bitters. Shake until the edges of the ice are smoothed.

2. Strain the cocktail into ice-filled cocktail glasses and garnish with a few cubes of mango before serving.

Extra Tip:

Don't confuse ginger beer and ginger ale, these two drinks are not the same thing! Ginger beer has a spicier flavor to it and ginger ale is much sweeter.

Chapter Three: 18 Hot Cocktails for Those Cold Winter Nights

"There's naught, no doubt, so much the spirit calms as rum and true religion."
– Lord Byron

In this chapter, you will learn how to make the following eighteen hot cocktail recipes:

- Candy Cane Hot Cocoa

- Whipped Cream Hot Chocolate

- Aged Hot Toddy

- Coffee with a Kick

- Buttered Hot Coffee

- Cocoa with a Kick

- Atomic Cider

- Bourbon Brandy Yuzu

- Cinnamon Coffee Cocktail

- Minted Cocoa

- Spiced Buttered Rum

- Dark Cinnamon Rum Hot Cocoa

- Almond Hot Coffee

- Spiced Bourbon Cider

- Jim's Hot Chocolate

- Buttered Clove Rum

- Cloved Whiskey

- Cinnamon Cocoa Cocktail

Candy Cane Hot Cocoa

Staple Liquor	Vodka
Flavor	Sweet

Ingredients

- 1 part vodka

- ½ part peppermint schnapps

- Hot chocolate of your choice

- Whipped cream

- Candy cane

- Mug

Let's Mix:

1. Make your hot chocolate as you usually would, making sure to leave room in the mug for your other ingredients.

2. Add your peppermint schnapps and vodka to the hot chocolate. Use your candy cane to stir your ingredients.

3. Garnish with whipped cream and hook your candy cane on the edge of your mug. Serve!

Extra Tip:

Add a festive garnish to your mug by crushing a piece of candy cane and sprinkling the pieces over the whipped cream on top of your drink.

Whipped Cream Hot Chocolate

Staple Liquor	Vodka
Flavor	Sweet

Ingredients

- 1 part whipped vodka

- 2 parts hot chocolate of your choice

- 1 maraschino cherry

- Whipped cream

- Milk chocolate shavings

- Mug

Let's Mix:

1. Make your hot chocolate as you would normally, leaving room in the mug for your other ingredients.

2. Add your whipped vodka and stir to mix.

3. Top with whipped cream and the chocolate shavings. Drop the cherry on top and serve!

Extra Tip:

Don't get carried away by adding more liquor to this drink. It can be easy to think there isn't enough liquor because of the sweetness of this recipe, but there is plenty!

Aged Hot Toddy

Staple Liquor	Rum
Flavor	Sweet

Ingredients

- 1 part aged dark rum

- 1 tsp. honey

- 1 oz. hot water

- 1 spiral lemon peel

- Mug

Let's Mix:

1. Begin by warming your mug by rinsing it well with boiling water. Make sure to empty out all of the water.

2. Add the lemon peel and honey to the bottom of your rinsed mug and top with the 1 oz. hot water. Stir these ingredients until the honey has melted into the water.

3. Pour the aged rum on top of the honey mixture and fill the rest of the mug with boiling water.

4. Stir well to mix and serve.

Extra Tip:

This is a great go-to drink for those winter nights or when you feel a head cold or flu coming on.

Coffee with a Kick

Staple Liquor	Irish Whiskey
Flavor	Malted

Ingredients

- 1 ½ parts 2 Gingers Whiskey

- 1 part hot coffee of your choice

- 1/8 part brown sugar

- Whipped cream

- Mug

Let's Mix:

1. Pour your coffee into a large coffee mug and add your whiskey.

2. Stir your brown sugar into your coffee mixture and then top with the whipped cream before serving.

Extra Tip:

Avoid using flavored coffees for this hot cocktail, rather, choose a single origin coffee bean with a strong but singular taste profile.

Buttered Hot Coffee

Staple Liquor	Cordials
Flavor	Sweet

Ingredients

- ¾ part coffee liqueur

- ¾ part butterscotch schnapps

- ¾ part Irish cream

- 1 cup hot coffee of your choice

- Whipped cream

- Butterscotch syrup

- Mug

Let's Mix:

1. Add your coffee to a large coffee mug, leaving room for the rest of your ingredients.

2. Add your Irish cream, coffee liqueur, and butterscotch schnapps. Stir gently to mix.

3. Top with whipped cream and lightly drizzle butterscotch syrup on top of the whipped cream before serving.

Extra Tip:

If you're not a fan of very sweet drinks, leave out the butterscotch syrup from this recipe, it can be a little too sweet for some.

Cocoa with a Kick

Staple Liquor	Bourbon
Flavor	Spicy, Sweet

Ingredients

- 2 parts bourbon whiskey

- ¼ part walnut liqueur

- ½ tbsp. unsweet cocoa powder

- ½ tbsp. sugar

- Pinch salt

- Pinch cayenne pepper

- Mug

Let's Mix:

1. Combine your cocoa powder, salt, sugar, and cayenne pepper. This results in your spiced hot cocoa mix.

2. Rinse your mug with boiling water to warm it thoroughly. Make sure the mug is completely empty and add the walnut liqueur and bourbon.

3. Make your hot cocoa by pouring hot water over the hot cocoa mix you made in step one.

4. Pour your prepared cocoa (2 parts) over the walnut liqueur and stir.

Extra Tip:

You can temper the spice in this spicy hot cocoa by playing with the level of cayenne pepper or adding a little chili pepper for garnish.

Atomic Cider

Staple Liquor	Vodka
Flavor	Sweet, Spicy

Ingredients

- 1 part Atomic Hot Vodka

- 1 cup hot apple cider

- Whipped cream

- Mug

Let's Mix:

1. Add the vodka to your mug and fill the rest of the mug with your prepared hot cider.

2. Garnish with whipped cream and serve.

Extra Tip:

If you can't get hold of Atomic Hot Vodka, you can go with any spiced vodka.

Bourbon Brandy Yuzu

Staple Liquor	Bourbon
Flavor	Sweet

Ingredients

- 1 part bourbon

- ¾ part apple brandy

- 5 parts hot water

- ½ part Yuzu juice

- ¼ cup Yuzu rind

- ½ cup honey

- 10 tbsp. sugar

- ½ cup water

- 1 ½ tsp. pectin

- 2 tbsp. Yuzu juice

- Mug

Let's Mix:

1. Begin by making a Yuzu honey. Add ½ cup water to the ¼ cup Yuzu rind and bring to a simmer on the stove. Once simmering, mix your 1 ½ tsp. pectin and 10 tbsp. sugar together and then stir into the simmering mixture. Let this mixture come to a boil before adding the ½ cup honey. Continue to stir until the mixture thickens and then add in 2 tbsp. Yuzu juice. Let this mixture continue to cook for a minute and then take off the heat.

2. Now that your Yuzu honey is made, take 2 tsp. of this honey mixture and mix together with 1 part bourbon, ¾ part apple brandy, 5 parts hot water, and ½ part Yuzu juice. Stir to combine and serve.

Extra Tip:

This is a unique flavored hot cocktail, I advise making it at home and trying it first before serving it at a cocktail party!

Cinnamon Coffee Cocktail

Staple Liquor	Vodka
Flavor	Sweet

Ingredients

- 1 part Cinnabon vodka

- 2 parts hot coffee

- Whipped cream

- Ground cinnamon

- 2 cinnamon sticks

- Mug

Let's Mix:

1. Make your coffee as you usually would and stir in your Cinnabon vodka. Stir well to mix.

2. Top with whipped cream and sprinkle cinnamon on top. Add the cinnamon sticks for garnish and serve.

Extra Tip:

Add a frothed milk instead of whipped cream on top of this cocktail if you want to cut the sweetness down a little.

Minted Cocoa

Staple Liquor	Cordials
Flavor	Sweet

Ingredients

- 1 part peppermint schnapps

- Hot chocolate

- 1 peppermint marshmallow

- Whipped cream

- Mug

Let's Mix:

1. Make your favorite hot chocolate as you usually would, making sure to leave space in your mug for the rest of your ingredients.

2. Add the peppermint schnapps to your hot chocolate and stir to mix well.

3. Garnish with whipped cream and add a peppermint marshmallow on top before serving!

Extra Tip:

If you can't find peppermint marshmallows, use regular marshmallows and sprinkle crushed candy cane pieces on top of your whipped cream.

Spiced Buttered Rum

Staple Liquor	Rum
Flavor	Sweet

Ingredients

- 1 ½ parts spiced rum

- 1 lb. brown sugar

- ½ lb. softened salted butter

- 2 tsp. nutmeg

- ½ tsp. allspice

- Dash ground clove

- 1 tsp. vanilla extract

- Mug

Let's Mix:

5. Add all of your ingredients in a mixing bowl except for your rum. Stir well to mix thoroughly or use a

hand mixer to combine. This will create a batter to use in this cocktail.

6. Fill a large coffee mug ¾ full with hot water and then stir in 2 hefty bar spoons of the batter that you made in step 1.

7. When the batter is dissolved completely in hot water, add in your rum and stir before serving.

Extra Tip:

Keep in mind that there will be plenty of batter when you follow this recipe, so it's not practical to make this cocktail for just one drink!

Dark Cinnamon Rum Hot Cocoa

Staple Liquor	Rum
Flavor	Sweet

Ingredients

- 1 part cinnamon rum

- 1 part barrel aged rum

- 2 parts hot chocolate

- 1 pinch chili powder

- 1 pinch salt

- Dash ground cinnamon

- Whipped cream

- Mug

Let's Mix:

1. In a small saucepan over medium heat, whisk together your ingredients while bringing them up to heat.

2. Once well mixed and warm, pour the drink into a mug and garnish with whipped cream before serving.

Extra Tip:

Add a little more garnish to this drink with a stick or two of cinnamon.

Almond Hot Coffee

Staple Liquor	Vodka
Flavor	Sweet

Ingredients

- 1 part amaretto vodka

- 1 part hot coffee

- Sliced toasted almonds

- Whipped cream

- Mug

Let's Mix:

1. Add your amaretto vodka to a large coffee mug.

2. Pour hot coffee prepared to your liking over the amaretto vodka and stir well to mix.

3. Top your mug with whipped cream and sprinkle a few of your almonds on top before serving.

Extra Tip:

Not a fan of using nuts as a garnish? You can grate milk chocolate on top of this cocktail and add a deliciously sweet touch instead.

Spiced Bourbon Cider

Staple Liquor	Bourbon
Flavor	Sweet

Ingredients

- 1 ¼ part bourbon

- Hot apple cider

- 1 pinch allspice

- 1 lemon slice

- 1 cinnamon stick

- Mug

Let's Mix:

1. Add your bourbon to a large mug and fill the rest of the mug with hot apple cider. Stir.

2. Add in just a dash of allspice and stir.

3. Add a cinnamon stick and a slice of lemon for garnish and serve.

Extra Tip:

Instead of sliced lemon, try garnishing this cocktail with a slice of dried apple to give it a more fall themed appearance.

Jim's Hot Cocoa

Staple Liquor	Bourbon
Flavor	Sweet

Ingredients

- 1 part Jim Beam Kentucky Fire

- 3 parts hot chocolate

- Mini marshmallows

- Whipped cream

- Mug

Let's Mix:

1. Fill a large mug ¾ full with your favorite brand of hot chocolate.

2. Fill the rest of the mug with your bourbon and stir well to mix.

3. Garnish with whipped cream and mini marshmallows before serving.

Extra Tip:

Prefer more of a savory flavor? Leave out the marshmallows and use a Mexican hot chocolate instead.

Buttered Clove Rum

Staple Liquor	Rum
Flavor	Sweet

Ingredients

- 2 cups rum

- ½ cup butter

- 2 cups brown sugar

- 1 cup sweet whipped cream

- 6 cloves

- 2 quarts hot water

- Pinch of salt

- Nutmeg

- 3 cinnamon sticks

- Mugs

Let's Mix:

1. Add the butter, salt, brown sugar, and hot water to a slow cooker. Stir to combine.

2. Throw the cloves and cinnamon sticks to the mixture and put the lid on the slow cooker. Cook on low heat for 5 hours.

3. After cooking, stir the rum into the ingredients, and pour into individual mugs.

4. Top each drink with whipped cream and sprinkle with nutmeg.

Extra Tip:

In lieu of using a slow cooker, you can simmer these ingredients on the stovetop and get your cocktails completed much faster.

Cloved Whiskey

Staple Liquor	Rum
Flavor	Sweet

Ingredients

- ¾ cup boiling water

- 1.5 oz. Irish whiskey

- 1 slice lemon

- 1 tbsp. sugar

- 8 cloves

- Mug

Let's Mix:

1. Take the cloves and push them into the peel of the lemon slice.

2. Add the sugar to a mug and pour the hot water over the sugar. Stir to dissolve the sugar completely.

3. Add the whiskey to the glass and throw the lemon slice on top.

4. Leave the drink to season itself for at least a minute before drinking.

Extra Tip:

Add a little honey to this drink if you need a little more sweetness. Just add to taste.

Cinnamon Cocoa Cocktail

Staple Liquor	Cordials
Flavor	Sweet

Ingredients

- 1 cup hot chocolate of your choice

- 1 part cinnamon schnapps liqueur

- Whipped cream

- Cinnamon

- Mug

Let's Mix:

1. Make your hot chocolate as you would normally, making sure to leave enough room for your other ingredients.

2. Add your liqueur to the mug and stir well to mix thoroughly.

3. Top each mug with whipped cream and a sprinkle of cinnamon before serving.

Extra Tip:

Instead of cinnamon, you can drizzle the top of this hot cocktail with chocolate syrup.

Chapter Four: 18 Tasty Non-Alcoholic Cocktails

"Drink moderately, for drunkenness neither keeps a secret nor observes a promise."
– Washington Irving

In this chapter, you will learn how to make the following delicious, but non-alcoholic cocktails:

- Cranberry Cooler

- Fruit Cream Soda

- Virgin Strawberry Mojito

- Coke and Grenadine

- Raspberry Fizz Bomb

- Cranberry Sparkle

- Virgin Mint Colada

- Lime and Coconut Virgin Martini

- Virgin Champagne Cocktail

- Sherbert Mojitos

- Ginger Cherry Virgin Cocktail

- Apple Citrus Cocktail

- Cucumber Grape Refresher

- Honey Watermelon Slushie

- Citrus Berry Cocktail

- Cranberry Apple Fizz

- Mango Refresher

- Sweet Grenadine

Cranberry Cooler

Staple Liquor	None
Flavor	Sweet, Fruity

Ingredients

- 1 part pineapple juice

- 2 parts cranberry juice

- 1 part orange juice

- 2 tbsp. lemon juice

- 1 can (12 fl.oz.) ginger ale

- 1 jar (4 oz.) maraschino cherries

- Orange slices

- Tall glass

Let's Mix:

1. Add your pineapple juice, cranberry juice, juice from the cherries, orange juice, and lemon juice to a large pitcher and stir to combine.

2. When ready to serve, pour in the ginger ale and stir.

3. Serve over ice with an orange slice and cherry on each glass.

Extra Tip:

Substitute bottled cherry juice for the maraschino cherry juice if you prefer, the flavor will still be just as good!

Fruit Cream Soda

Staple Liquor	None
Flavor	Sweet, Fruity

Ingredients

- 8 fl. oz. carbonated water

- ¾ fl. oz. watermelon syrup

- ¾ fl. oz. passion fruit syrup

- 1 fl. oz. half and a half

- 1 sprig fresh mint

- Tall glass

Let's Mix:

1. Fill your tall glass with ice and then fill the glass 2/3 full with your carbonated water.

2. Add your fruit syrups over the carbonated water and then top with the half and half.

3. Stir just before serving and top with a sprig of fresh mint.

Extra Tip:

If you are short on half and half or simply don't have any, you can make this cocktail without it but you will lose some of the texture and milkiness.

Virgin Strawberry Mojito

Staple Liquor	None
Flavor	Sweet, Fruity

Ingredients

- 8 quartered strawberries

- 3 cups carbonated water

- 2 quartered limes

- 1 cup sugar

- 1 bunch of fresh mints

- Fresh mint leaves for garnish

- Wine glass

Let's Mix:

1. Juice your limes into a large pitcher and drop the juiced limes into the pitcher when you have finished.

2. In a bowl, use a muddler to muddle together your mint and strawberries. Add this mixture to the pitcher with your limes along with your sugar.

3. Using a long-handled spoon, stir your ingredients as you add your club soda. Keep stirring until the sugar has dissolved completely.

4. Dip the rim of your glass in water and then sugar before adding ice. Pour your cocktail over the ice and serve with a fresh mint leaf for garnish.

Extra Tip:

Don't skip muddling the mint and strawberry together! Muddling helps to release the flavors of the mint leaves and combine them with the fresh strawberry juice.

Coke and Grenadine

Staple Liquor	None
Flavor	Sweet

Ingredients

- 1 can cola

- 1 tbsp. lime juice

- 1 tbsp. cherry grenadine syrup

- 1 lemon zest twist

- Tall glass

Let's Mix:

1. Fill your tall glass with ice and pour the grenadine and lime juice into the bottom of the glass.

2. Top the glass with your cola and stir.

3. Garnish with the lemon zest twist before serving.

Extra Tip:

Make sure to use a good quality cola in this recipe, remember, the quality of your "mixers" is just as important as the quality of alcohol in cocktails. This is even more important in alcohol-free cocktails.

Raspberry Fizz Bomb

Staple Liquor	None
Flavor	Sweet

Ingredients

- 1.5 fl. oz. raspberry syrup

- 1 quartered lime

- 8 fl. oz. carbonated water

- 1 fresh lime wedge

- Tall glass

Let's Mix:

1. Fill your glass with ice and squeeze the juice from your quartered lime into your glass. Throw the juiced lime pieces into the glass.

2. Add the carbonated water into the glass and stir.

3. Top the glass with your raspberry syrup.

4. Add a wedge of lime on the side of the glass for garnish before serving.

Extra Tip:

This is a non-alcoholic cocktail that can be made with any range of fruit syrups, you can even make a rainbow selection with an array of different syrups.

Cranberry Sparkle

Staple Liquor	None
Flavor	Sweet, Fruity

Ingredients

- 8 fl. oz. cranberry juice cocktail

- 2 fl. oz. carbonated water

- 1 lime wedge

- Large wine glass

Let's Mix:

1. Fill your glass with ice and pour your cranberry juice on top of the ice.

2. Top the glass with sparkling water and stir.

3. Garnish the side of the glass with a lime wedge and serve.

Extra Tip:

Want a little something sweeter? Replace the carbonated water in this recipe with lemon lime soda instead.

Virgin Mint Colada

Staple Liquor	None
Flavor	Sweet

Ingredients

- 6 oz. pineapple juice

- 6 fl. oz. coconut milk

- 2 tbsp. almond syrup

- 3 juiced limes

- Club soda

- 4 pinches nutmeg

- 4 slices fresh lime

- 4 sprigs fresh mint

- Tall glass

Let's Mix:

1. Fill a pitcher 1/3 the way full with ice. Pour your coconut milk, pineapple juice, almond syrup, and lime juice over the ice. Stir to mix.

2. Strain the contents of the pitcher into 4 glasses and top off each glass with the club soda.

3. Sprinkle nutmeg on top of each glass and hook a lime slice on the side of each glass. Drop a sprig of mint on top and serve!

Extra Tip:

You can make this an alcoholic cocktail by adding 2 oz. of rum to the recipe.

Lime and Coconut Virgin Martini

Staple Liquor	None
Flavor	Sweet

Ingredients

- ½ cup unsweet coconut cream

- 2 cups pineapple juice

- ½ cup lime juice

- 1 lime cut into 8 pieces

- Martini glasses

Let's Mix:

1. Fill a large drink pitcher with ice and pour the coconut cream, pineapple juice, and lime juice over it.

2. Put a lid on the pitcher or cover securely and shake to mix your ingredients.

3. Strain your cocktail into glasses and garnish each glass with a wedge of lime.

Extra Tip:

Instead of lime garnish, you can sprinkle a little-sweetened coconut on top of this cocktail instead.

Virgin Champagne Cocktail

Staple Liquor	None
Flavor	Sweet

Ingredients

- 46 fl. oz. cranberry juice

- 46 fl. oz. pineapple juice

- 12 fl. oz. frozen orange juice concentrate

- 2 quarts ginger ale

- Orange zest

- Tall glasses

Let's Mix:

1. In a large drink pitcher add enough ice to fill the pitcher half full.

2. Add the rest of the ingredients except for the orange zest to the pitcher and stir to mix.

3. Pour into individual glasses and sprinkle the top of each cocktail with orange zest before serving.

Extra Tip:

This recipe makes around 20 servings so if you're not looking to entertain, make sure that you scale down the ingredients!

Sherbert Mojitos

Staple Liquor	None
Flavor	Sweet

Ingredients

- 1 cup lime juice

- 3 cups water

- 8 cups club soda

- 1 ½ cups white sugar

- 2 cups soft lime sherbert

- 2 cups chopped mint leaves

- Sliced lime for garnish

- Rocks glasses

Let's Mix:

1. In a large microwave-safe bowl, combine your sugar and 2 cups of water and heat for 5 minutes.

2. Stir your heated sugar water and mix in the mint leaves. Let these leaves steep for 5 minutes before straining them out of the mixture.

3. In a large pitcher, mix together the lime juice, 1 cup water, and lime sherbert until combined.

4. Add the mint water mixture to the pitcher and top with club soda. Mix well.

5. Fill individual glasses with ice and pour the cocktail over the ice filled glasses. Garnish each glass with slices of fresh lime.

Extra Tip:

It is very important to get a good quality sherbert for this cocktail. Cheap sherbert ice creams can be bitter and leave a bad aftertaste.

Ginger Cherry Virgin Cocktail

Staple Liquor	None
Flavor	Sweet

Ingredients

- 1 cup ginger ale

- 3 tbsp. frozen cherry juice concentrate

- Rocks glass

Let's Mix:

1. Add the cherry juice to a glass filled with ice.

2. Top the glass off with ginger ale and stir thoroughly to mix.

Extra Tip:

If you can't find cherry concentrate, you can substitute similarly flavored fruit like raspberry concentrate instead.

Apple Citrus Cocktail

Staple Liquor	None
Flavor	Sweet, Fruity

Ingredients

- 1 cup pineapple juice

- 1-quart apple juice

- 1 cup orange juice

- ¼ cup lemon juice

- 1 sprig fresh mint leaves

- Orange slices

- Tall glasses

Let's Mix:

1. Fill a large pitcher halfway full with ice.

2. Pour the pineapple juice, apple juice, orange juice, and lemon juice into the pitcher and stir.

3. Fill each serving glass with ice and strain the cocktail mixture into each glass.

4. Top each cocktail with a mint leaf and slip a slice of orange onto the side of each glass and serve!

Extra Tip:

To make this an alcoholic cocktail, just add a splash of rum and you're good to go!

Cucumber Grape Refresher

Staple Liquor	None
Flavor	Fruity

Ingredients

- 12 fl. oz. white grape juice concentrate

- 3 quarts water

- .14 oz. instant lemonade powder

- 1 sliced lemon

- ½ cucumber sliced

- Tall glasses

Let's Mix:

1. Fill a large drinking pitcher halfway with ice.

2. Add the water, grape juice concentrate, and lemonade powder to the pitcher and stir well.

3. Pour the cocktail into individual glasses and garnish each glass with a slice of lemon and a few cucumber slices dropped in the drink.

Extra Tip:

Replace the water in this recipe with carbonated water to get a sparkling cocktail.

Honey Watermelon Slushie

Staple Liquor	None
Flavor	Sweet

Ingredients

- 2 cups seedless cubed watermelon

- 1 tsp. honey

- 1 cup lemon-lime soda

- Thin watermelon wedges

- Tall glasses

Let's Mix:

1. Add a couple of handfuls of crushed ice to a blender. Add the watermelon on top of the ice and pulse until the watermelon mixture is slushy.

2. Once your mixture is slushy, add in the honey and soda and blend again for a few seconds until mixed thoroughly.

3. Serve in tall glasses with a small, thin slice of watermelon on the side of each glass.

Extra Tip:

This cocktail can be made without the lemon-lime soda, but be sure to add a little sugar and a squeeze of lemon instead to round out the flavor profile.

Citrus Berry Cocktail

Staple Liquor	None
Flavor	Sweet, Fruity

Ingredients

- 12 fl. oz. lemon-lime soda

- 12 fl. oz. cranberry-raspberry juice

- Fresh raspberries

- Tall glasses

Let's Mix:

1. Fill a large pitcher halfway full with ice. Pour the juice and soda over the ice and stir to mix.

2. Strain the cocktail into two glasses and garnish each with a single fresh raspberry.

Extra Tip:

This non-alcoholic cocktail can be made with any fruit juice mixture but tastes best with cranberry juice combinations.

Cranberry Apple Fizz

Staple Liquor	None
Flavor	Sweet, Fruity

Ingredients

- 1 fl. oz. carbonated water

- 6 fl. oz. cranberry apple juice

- Apple slice

- Tall glass

Let's Mix:

1. Fill a tall glass with ice and mix the two juices over the ice. Stir.

2. Garnish each glass with a slice of apple and serve.

Extra Tip:

Don't have any apples handy? Garnish the glasses with a thin wedge of lime instead!

Mango Refresher

Staple Liquor	None
Flavor	Sweet, Fruity

Ingredients

- ½ cup orange juice

- ¼ cup mango juice

- 1 ¼ cup ginger ale

- 1 peeled, chunked mango

- 2 ice cubes

- ½ oz. simple sugar

- 1/8 cup lime juice

- Orange slices

- Tall Glasses

Let's Mix:

1. Use a muddler to mix together your sugar and lime juice.

2. Put the mango into a blender and blend until smooth. Add the lime juice/sugar mixture and orange juice to the blended mango and blend again until smooth.

3. Add the ice cubes and ginger ale to the blender and blend again until the ice cubes are crushed completely.

4. Pour into 3 glasses and add a slice of orange on the side of each glass before serving.

Extra Tip:

It's important to use mangos at peak ripeness for this cocktail mixture. If you are unable to find ripe mangos, use thawed frozen mango instead.

Sweet Grenadine

Staple Liquor	None
Flavor	Sweet, Fruity

Ingredients

- 1 part lemon-lime soda

- 1 part orange juice

- Splash of grenadine

- Orange slices

- Tall glasses

Let's Mix:

1. Add ice to two tall glasses and put a splash of grenadine into each glass.

2. In a pitcher, combine the lemon-lime soda and orange juice and mix together thoroughly. Once mixed, pour over the grenadine ice in both glasses.

3. Garnish each glass with a slice of orange before serving.

Extra Tip:

Make sure to check the grenadine that you use in non-alcoholic cocktails to ensure that it doesn't contain any alcohol. Some variations of grenadine do contain alcohol!

Best Practices & Common Mistakes

In the first chapter of the book, I covered a few important tips to making sure that your craft cocktails turn out right the first time! In this section, I want to touch on a few more do's and don'ts to help you along your way.

Do's

Perfect one before you move on!

Before you start mixing up all kinds of cocktails for your friends, start with one recipe and perfect it. Mix that drink, taste it, and practice your hand at it until you have really perfected the recipe and mixing technique. One great cocktail is far better than six mediocre ones!

Keep things uniform

The best liquors to mix for most amateur bartenders or cocktail makers are mid-range liquors. That is, affordable, but not cheap. Keep things uniform when mixing drinks by purchasing mixing ingredients of similar quality. For example, a decent liquor can be tainted by mixing it with a generic brand soda. Keeping your ingredients uniform will avoid ingredients degrading each other and ruining your end flavor.

Use your own time to experiment

If you get the bug and want to start mixing your own craft cocktails, do it on your own time. Don't use a cocktail party as an opportunity to try out "new ideas." No one wants to volunteer to be the subject of experimentation and no good party host should turn their guests into guinea pigs!

Don'ts

Don't substitute!

If a recipe calls for lemon and you only have lime, DON'T SUBSTITUTE! Every element of a cocktail is perfectly balanced for flavor. When you substitute one ingredient for another, you are essentially making an entirely new drink. This is fine if you're experimenting, but if you're having a cocktail or dinner party, it's not the time to get inventive!

Don't skimp on the ice

I already mentioned the importance of good quality ice, but it's also important that you have plenty of it! Most amateur bartenders underestimate the amount of ice they will need to mix cocktails for a party. It is far easier to deal with having too much ice than it is to deal with having too little.

Don't get fancy

Chances are that you aren't a professional mixologist and your friends won't expect you to be one either. So, skip over the fancy pouring and mixing tricks and focus instead on your technique. Your aim is to impress your guests with the best-mixed drink possible, not to impress them with your mixing skills. If you want to perfect something, make it your measuring skills, it's much more impressive to balance a drink's flavor profile.

Conclusion

I hope that you have enjoyed reading this book as much as I enjoyed the research that went into writing it. I also hope that you give each recipe the time it deserves as you learn to mix each cocktail well before moving on to the next. Remember, perfecting one drink is the key to beginning your journey as a successful mixologist!

Bonus: Your FREE Gift

FREE **VIP** ACCESS

As a token of our appreciation, please take advantage of the **FREE Gift** - a lifetime **VIP Membership** at our book club.

Follow the link below to download your FREE books:

http://bit.ly/vipbookclub

As a VIP member, you will get an instant **FREE** access to exclusive new releases and bestselling books.

11928085R00078